Unlocking the Neck

UNDERSTANDING THE GUITAR WITH THE
FIVE-POSITION CAGED SYSTEM

DANIEL MYLOTTE

©2016 Daniel Mylotte

www.DanMylotte.com

Cover photo courtesy of Chris Lasher

Table of Contents

Chapter 1: Five of Everything
Chapter 2: Chords Become Scales
Chapter 3: How to Practice
Chapter 4: Pentatonic
Chapter 5: Arpeggios
Chapter 6: Making it Stick

Introduction

The guitar is one of the easiest instruments for a total beginner to make music with. At the same time, the interface is one of the harder ones to fully understand and master. Most students never do master it. If you have been playing for months or years and still have no idea what those note names are or why your fingers go on those frets to make that sound, you are not alone. In fact, this is what guitar playing is like for the average student. It's a process of mimicking what they've seen, heard, or read somewhere. Understanding seems to come much later or not at all.

Not that there's anything wrong with that! Plenty of players are perfectly content to enjoy making music with this limited understanding and have no need to strain their brains trying to make sense of it all. If you're reading this, though, you're probably not one of those people.

You poked around online and if you're smart you found a teacher or at least bought a book. You struggled through it for a while and probably learned a little bit but ultimately you ended up feeling like you're still not getting it. You reached the point I call "the plateau." In your defense, it probably is less about your inadequacies than it is about the lack of a clear system for unlocking the neck of the guitar. This is that system. I didn't invent it, but I'm going to go on record saying you will not find a clearer and more thorough presentation of how and why it works than the one in this book.

The objective of this book is to give you the tools to unlock the entire neck of the guitar and play anything anywhere, with no limitations regarding positions, fingerings, patterns or anything else. But we are going to use fingerings, patterns, and positions to get there. Along the way you are going to fill in some missing knowledge and probably advance your overall skill level quite a bit.

This is the path to the kind of fluid and effortless playing you see demonstrated by the master players. They seem to transcend scale shapes and play anywhere they want. Often it appears they aren't "in a position" or "using a shape." And it's possible they really aren't thinking about that at all. But I would bet my antique Gibson that they can "see" the key on the fretboard, regardless of whether they're thinking about patterns anymore. At some point they almost definitely did. And let's face it, these shapes are just the way the guitar is played. Once you learn them you're going to recognize them underlying so much of what you already know.

What Is It?

The Five Position System (frequently referred to as the CAGED system) uses five common forms to play a single chord sound up the neck in five places. Then seven-note major scale forms are derived from the chord forms. From here, all the other things you might need are built in conjunction with those scales: pentatonics, arpeggios, intervals, and so on. This means that the only memorization you will be doing revolves around 5 chords, all of which you probably already know.

What Is It Not?

The five position system is not modes. You don't need to learn more scale patterns in order to play modes. You can use the same ones in this system. Modes should exist in your mind and in your ears. Learning patterns for modes is a waste of time. For one thing, you'll have seven patterns instead of five, which is unnecessary. Even with five there is some overlap on the neck. If you must learn a pattern for the modes I'm not going to tell you that's wrong, it's just not worth the trouble in my opinion.

This is not a book about theory. While I'll make occasional references to theory concepts, most of them are not crucial to using this book. It wouldn't hurt to go learn some theory, though. Later on

I'll try to link to some of the videos on the Guitar Wisdom YouTube channel that might be helpful

The CAGED system is not going to make you an instant guitar god. It's not a "trick" that you learn in a five minute video. It will give you a pathway to playing more effective lead parts and a framework for improvising, but this will take considerable time. In the meantime, you will find that things you've already learned will begin to make more sense. Most importantly, you will stop relying on rote memorization. No longer will your performances be based on "My finger goes here, and then it goes here." That is not how a master musician approaches their instrument.

How long will it take?

Your ears should be leading you, not your fingers. Learning this system will begin to create a better connection between your intellectual understanding of music and your ability to hear it from an analytical and creative perspective. This will take time, and most of us don't have enough time.

I started using the Berklee guitar method with a teacher when I was 14. It teaches this system, but in a far more obtuse way. I learned patterns, played exercises, and definitely benefitted from it. But I was far from understanding the neck the way I do now. Later, in music school, when I was about 20, my teacher Tomo Fujita looked at me one day and said, "you don't understand the CAGED system, do you?"

I said, "what's that?" It wasn't just that I had never heard it referred to this way. Also, the concept of "a system" had not sunk in. Somehow, despite all that study, the grasp of the five positions as a cohesive approach to the whole neck still eluded me. I attribute this to the fact that the Berklee method fails to tie the scales to the chord shapes and present it in a way that makes that big picture come into focus. The information is there, it's just not explained that much. It takes a really great teacher to unlock that for you, and Tomo was a really great teacher.

He spent the rest of the semester making sure I grasped the system the way I do now. Within six months or so I had made sense of it and could see the whole neck as a single key. This was transformative. Granted, I already had many years of very focused study under my belt. And I was a full time music student practicing many hours a day! But I strongly feel that this system is very accessible to the average player if they take the time to learn it carefully. Most students of this method will have considerable experience by the time they need this material. Chances are you've played almost all of these forms and patterns before. Just like me sitting in Tomo's lesson room, what you need is the perspective to see the big picture. It's easier than you think, if you just keep working on it.

Give it a month and I promise you'll start seeing benefits. A year or two of solid study should completely revolutionize your playing and understanding of the instrument.

How To Use This Book

You're probably reading this on a small, handheld screen. In an effort to make this book as useful as possible I've created an archive of all the diagrams and examples in a pdf on my website

http://danmylotte.com/guitarwisdom/unlock/

so you can view them on a computer screen or print them as necessary. There are also playalong examples that will be linked from YouTube. They're in a playlist so you don't have to keep opening links.

It's entirely possible that you will have a Kindle, a phone, a computer, and a stack of papers all performing useful functions at the same time. This is good! If you find it overwhelming you can read first and come back to the examples with guitar in hand later, maybe using a computer to handle some of the playback. Some devices can read the text to you so give that a shot with the diagram printouts in hand if you find the multiple devices difficult to manage.

Browsing and indexing in eBooks has always been an annoying thing for me. I've tried to create a very usable table of contents, but I can't really help the limitations of the format. It's a trade-off for the accessibility. If this was a print book on a shelf somewhere you probably wouldn't have found it.

You are going to go back and forth a lot and I apologize in advance for the difficulty of doing this on a screen. Multiple devices or printing diagrams are the way to go here. It's absolutely useless to do the exercises in each chapter only once and move on. It should be weeks and weeks before you get to the material at the end so plan on re-tracing your steps again and again. For my part, I've done my best to make this the most elegantly formatted electronic publication in existence. I hope it helps.

Neck diagrams in this book are written in the standard right hand, horizontal, "I'm looking down at the neck in my hands" way. All examples are both tabbed and notated. I'm a firm believer in standard notation, probably because my formative musical training was on piano and winds. This doesn't mean you're forced to read it, but it wouldn't hurt to be able to identify notes on the treble clef at some point in your musical career.

I use the words "form," "pattern," and "shape" interchangeably to refer to the same thing. I also introduce terms from time to time and try to offer brief explanations where they're useful. But sometimes you may find a term that you don't recognize and isn't really explained. I think this is a good thing. This is like being in music school. A lot of what is going on is over your head and you can't absorb it all, but everything was new to you at one time. When you hear it again it will sink in a little more. If only there was a way you could easily look that stuff up...

Chapter 1: Five of Everything

Why five? That's all you need. Also, those are all the open chord shapes there are. Think about it. Can you come up with a unique open chord besides C, A, G, E, and D?

So there are five positions, five chords, five scales, five everything. No matter what key we're talking about, you'll only ever need these five positions to play it all over the neck. The positions are built around the chord shapes you know as C, A, G, E, and D. Yes they spell a word. It so happens that this word is also the order they are sequenced in to move up the neck, although the starting chord (the one in the lowest position) will vary based on the key you're in.

We can do this in C to show how they spell CAGED.

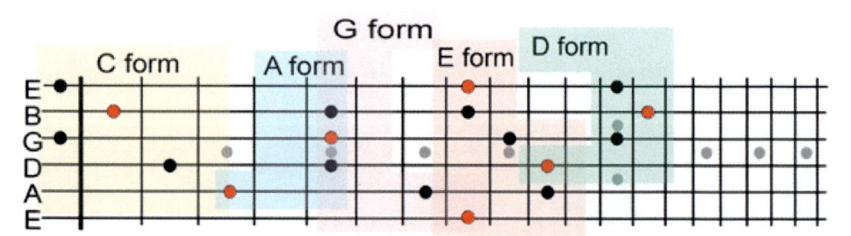

If we try another key you'll see they cycle through the same order from a different starting point

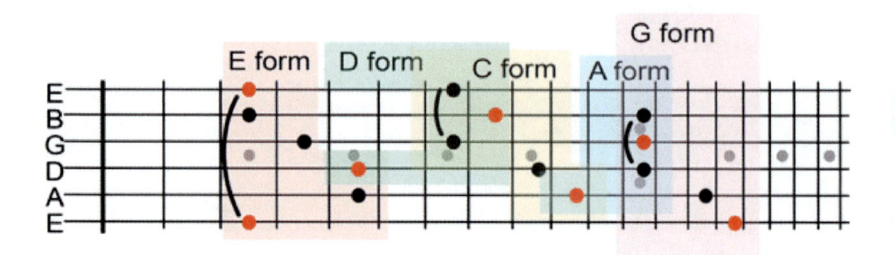

Making Barre Chords

Before we can use the five positions we have to be able to convert the open chord forms into barre chords. In some cases this results in a very useful chord shape. The E and A chord forms are cornerstones of rhythm guitar playing and you've almost definitely used them, probably extensively, to play chord accompaniments. I find the C shape to be useful as well, although considerably less common. You can get some mileage out of the G shape here and there. The D form, however, is almost worthless in terms of functional guitar playing. It's not worth spending time trying to master this shape. So why is it here?

We aren't actually that interested in playing these chord shapes the way you normally play chords in songs. I really don't care if you can ever get a good sound out of the C, G, and D forms (although, as stated, the E and A forms are crucial to rhythm guitar). Rather, we are trying to use them as markers for where the scale shapes are going to go later. Don't get too hung up on making these sound good. Simply use them as the guideposts to where each position is located on the neck for a given key.

We are really trying to establish the locations of the positions so that we can understand where the scales go. When we get there, we'll spend considerable time practicing them. You won't hear me say this often, but for now it's fine to just get a loose grasp on the chord side of things and go on without making them sound good.

Open Chords>Barre Chords

An open chord uses open strings in open position, meaning all the fretted notes are played within the first four frets (really the first three). A barre chord, however, uses no open strings. For this reason it can be moved, or transposed, up and down the neck. Obviously, this is more useful because it can be used to create that chord sound up and down the neck on any of the twelve notes (you know there are twelve notes, right?) instead of just the one sound in open position. If you try to move open chord shapes weird things will happen because only some of the notes will move.

To convert open chords to barre chords we have to adjust the fingerings so that the open string notes can be covered by a finger, usually stretched or "barred" across multiple strings. Here's how that looks for each of these five chord shapes. We'll move each of the open chords up a few frets to compare them.

C chord - Open

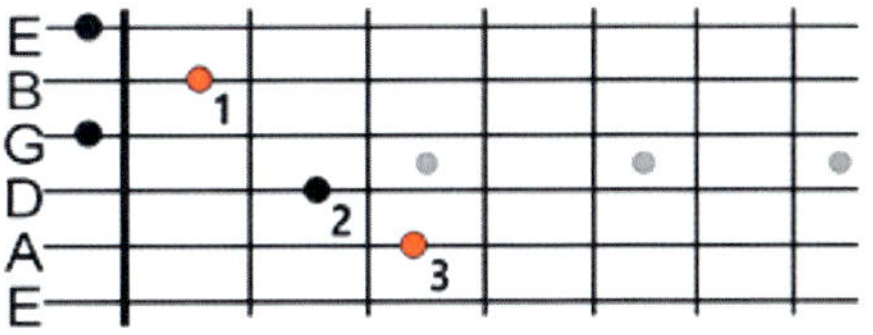

C form - Barre

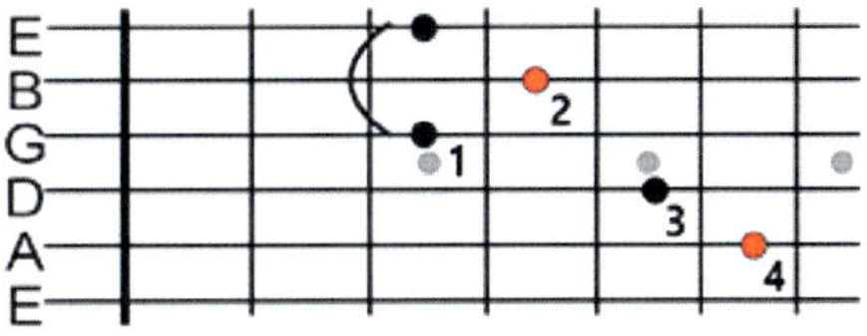

A chord - open

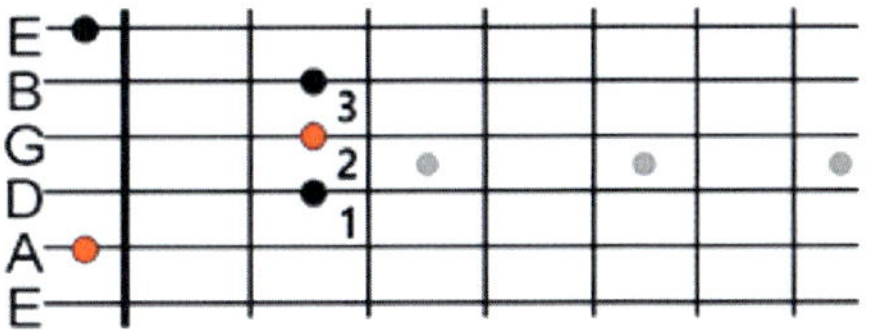

A form - barre

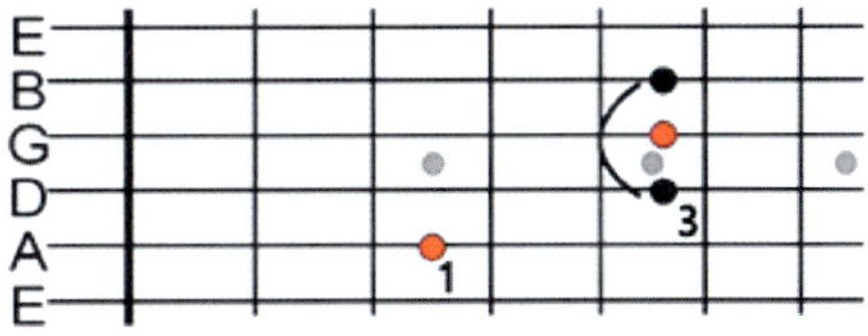

G chord - open

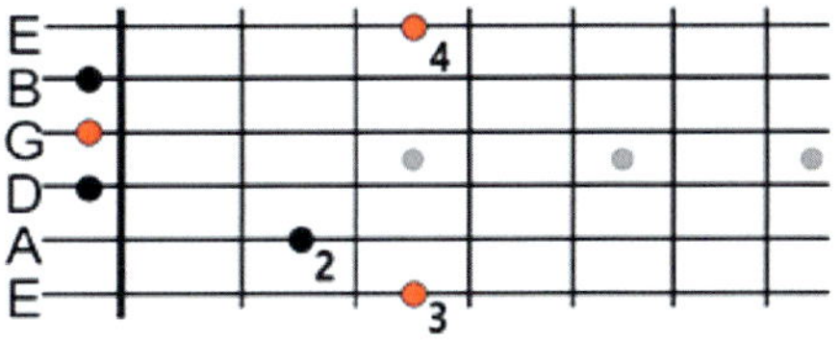

G form - barre

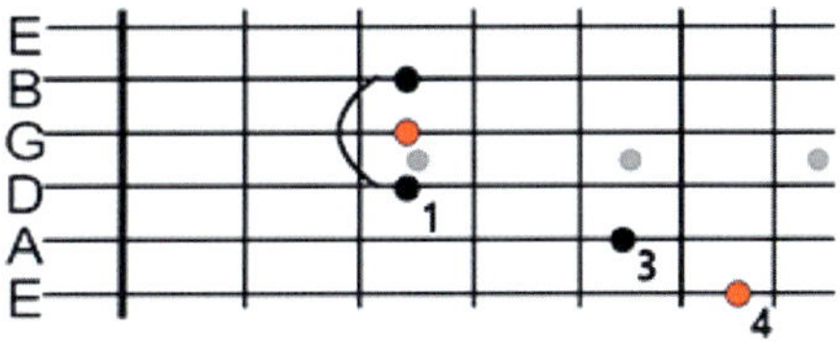

E chord - open

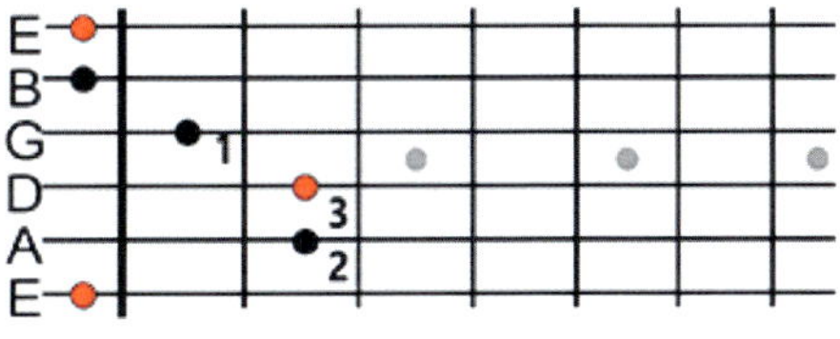

E form - barre

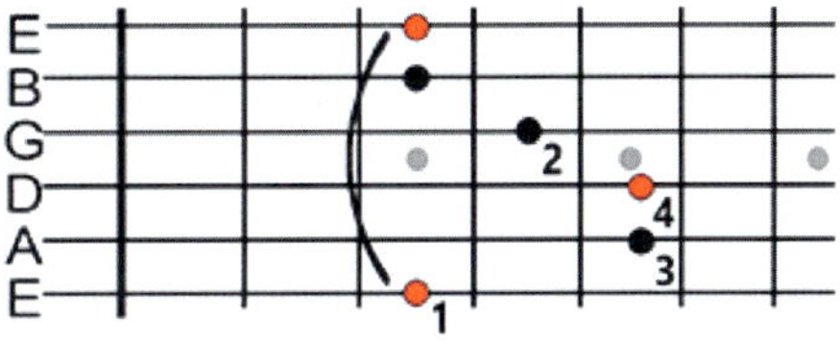

D chord - open

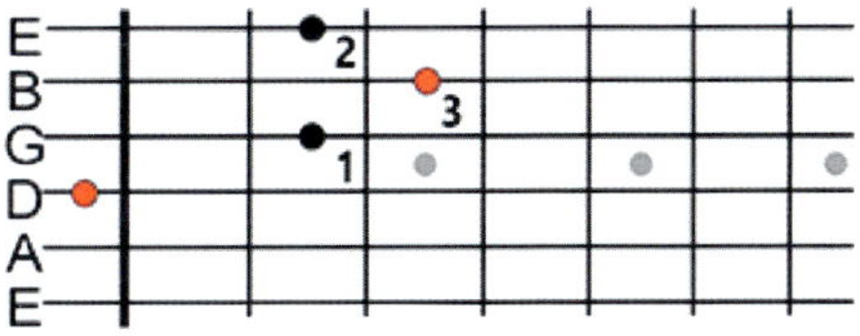

D form - barre

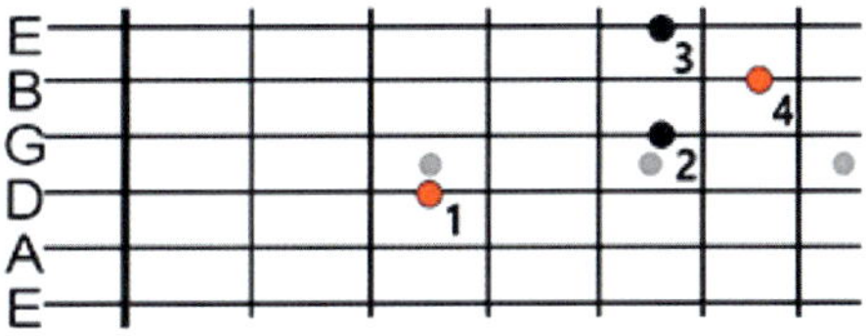

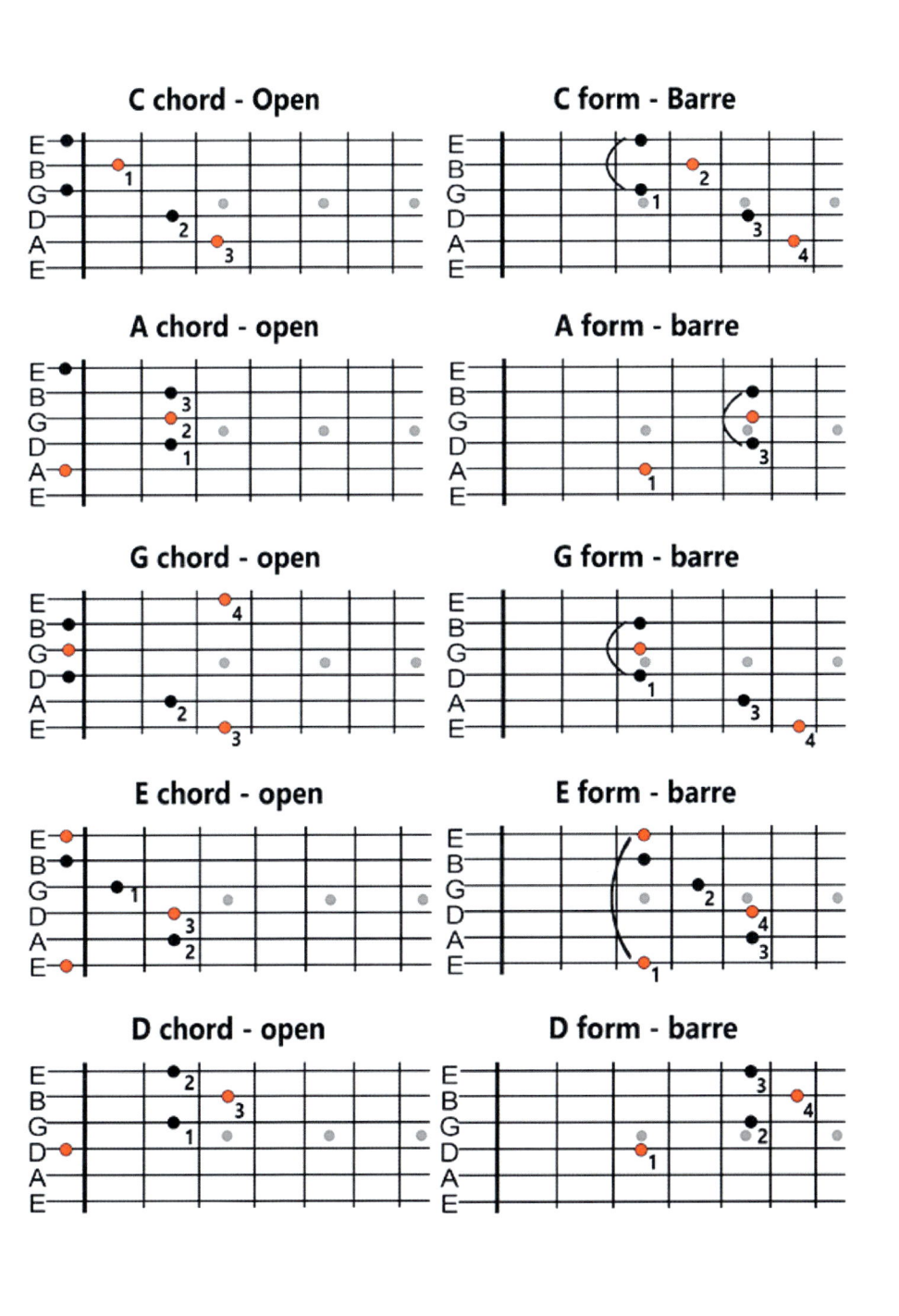

Notice that the D form doesn't actually have any barre the way I've written it. But the "barre" label still conveys the idea that you can move this shape up and down. Take a few minutes to get the hang of any of these shapes that are new to you. Again, don't worry if you're struggling with some of them. They don't have to be perfect in order to move on.

Sometimes you have to make sacrifices when you convert the open shape to a barre shape. It's often not possible to get all the notes covered when you have to make fingers do the work the open strings were doing. Some people will contort their hands to try get the first string to sound on the A form and G form. I don't think it's worth it. Just play them the way I've written them here.

Cycling Up the Neck

Let's start by doing this exactly the way the CAGED name describes it, from C, in C. It's very important at this point to understand that what we're about to do is play *a single major chord sound* in five different places on the neck. We are going to move these five shapes into the place on the neck where they all give us the sound of a C major triad (a triad is a three note chord sound stacked in intervals of thirds).

Another important thing to note is that when we do this process for the keys C, A, G, E, or D, the cycle will start with that open chord shape, not a barre chord. For the other seven keys all the shapes will be barre chords.

One last thing. Start categorizing these shapes according to which string the roots are on. E and G shapes have sixth string roots. A and C have fifth string roots. D has a fourth string root (although you'll see later that when we convert this shape to a scale the root moves onto the sixth string with the E and G forms).

C form

So in C, we start with the open C chord that you probably learned the first day or week you picked up a guitar. The C form, whether open or barred, has its root on the fifth string. The roots here are labeled with red dots (lighter gray if you are not on a color device).

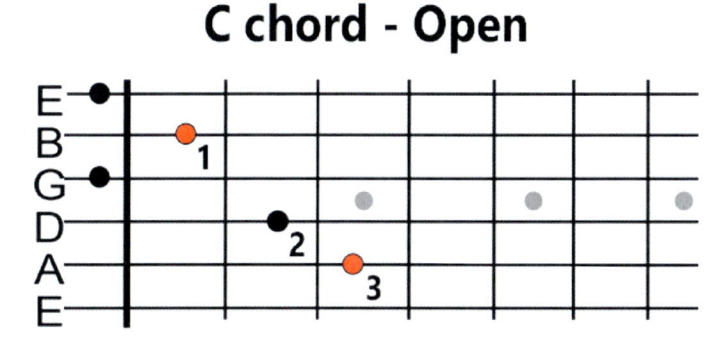

C chord - Open

A form

To move up to the next position it's helpful to think of certain notes in the form as a pivot point or marker for where to start building the next shape from. Between the C and A forms, that pivot point is the lowest root on the fifth string. The fifth string root of the C form is also the starting point for the A form, but the shape moves to the frets above it instead of below it the way you saw in the C form. I'll circle the pivot points for each shift.

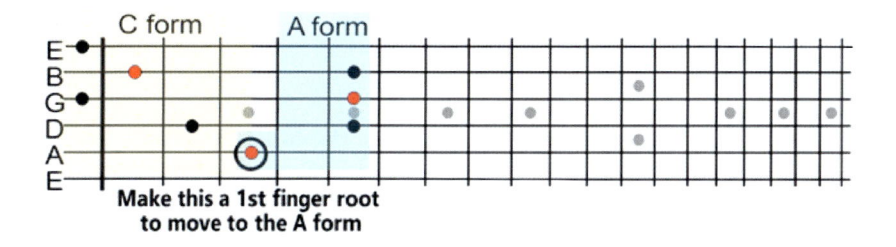

Make this a 1st finger root to move to the A form

You can see that the A form covers the next section of neck above the C form. Go back and forth between the two shapes. While they're not identical sounds, you can hear that they are both clearly the same C major chord because they contain only the notes C, E, and G. If you need some help on filling in the gaps in your theory knowledge you might want to have a look at the theory lessons on my YouTube channel:

https://goo.gl/PY5mZh

G form

After A is G. The notes of the third finger barre in the A form are the pivot point now. Barre those same notes instead with the first finger and you have the beginnings of the G form.

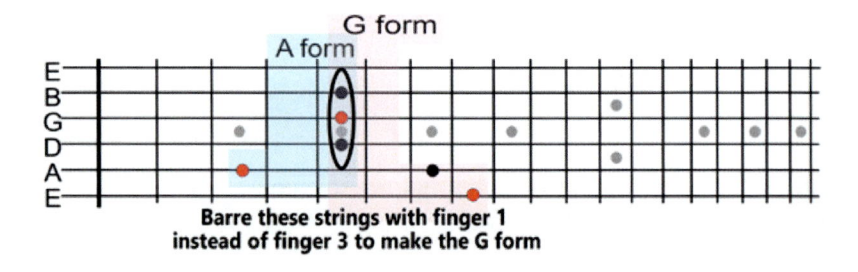

Barre these strings with finger 1 instead of finger 3 to make the G form

At this point we've started to use the sixth string as the location of the lowest root. This is another key concept. Roots are going to be found on the fifth or sixth string, and the various forms will be allowing you to play on either side of that root as the given musical situation requires.

E form

With the G form, the fourth finger played the sixth string root. To pivot to the E form, play that same sixth string root with the first finger instead. Then lay if flat to create the barre foundation for the E form.

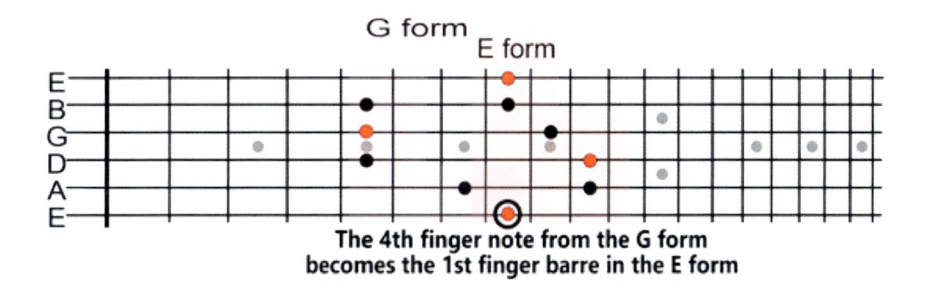

G form
E form

The 4th finger note from the G form becomes the 1st finger barre in the E form

D form

Now for the oddball D form. Not only is the form very dificult to finger, but this one goes against what I just said about fifth and sixth string roots. You'll see the root here is on the fourth string. The reason I stand by my previous statement is that when we create the scale shape for the D form it will go back to being a sixth string root.

You might know that the E form and A form have power chords embedded in them if you take the barre out. If you know anything about power chords you might know that the first and fourth fingers create an octave. So the fourth finger note in the E form is also a root. That is the pivot note to move into the D form. Put your first finger where your fourth finger was for the E form. Now try to get the rest of the D form in place.

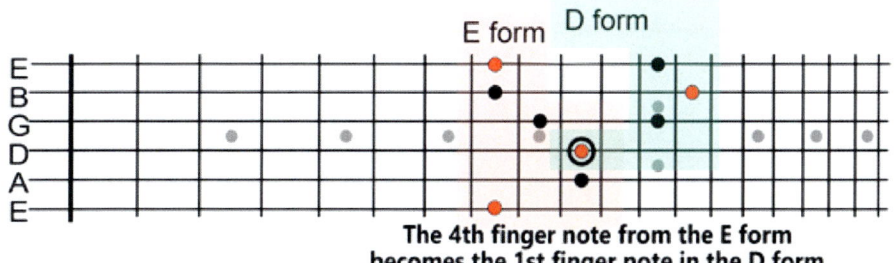

E form D form

The 4th finger note from the E form becomes the 1st finger note in the D form

Rinse and Repeat

Getting to the C form is easiest if you match up the triangle part of the D form with the same shape in the C form. Once you've done this you've made it back to where you started, but an octave higher. If you can squeeze your fingers into the smaller frets you could keep going through the cycle again.

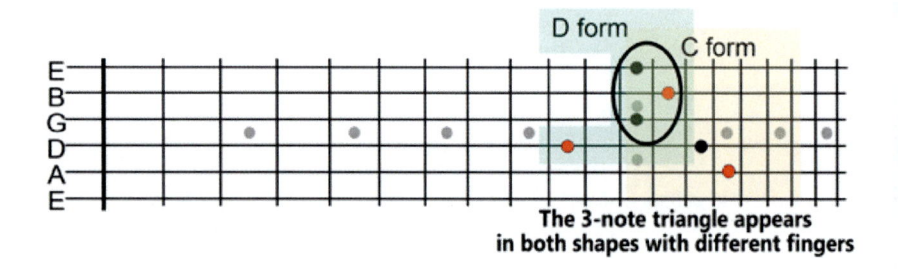

The 3-note triangle appears in both shapes with different fingers

A different key

Let's look at the cycle in G this time and talk about how you're going to identify the starting chord shape. As I said earlier, if you're in one of the keys that has its own CAGED shape (which G is) you just start with that open chord. So we could just start with an open G chord and follow the cycle through E-D-C-A.

Here's what that looks like on the neck. As you play through this series make sure to walk yourself through the pivot points from one shape to the next so you begin to internalize those connections. It looks a little overwhelming to see this all on the neck at once but if you pay attention to where the roots are you should be able to figure this out. If you get frustrated, go back and do the C cycle a few more times.

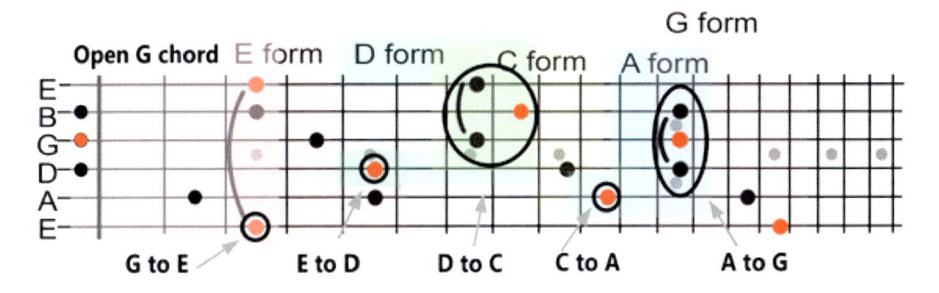

Finding the Start Point for Other Keys

If you happen to be doing this series in the keys of C, A, G, E, or D you have it easy. Just start from the open chord shape for that key. If you are not in the key of C, A, G, E, or D you have to do more work to figure out where the starting point is. Since only the D form has a root on the 4th string, you want to begin your search for the root on strings five or six. If you aren't already somewhat familiar with identifying notes on these strings, now is as good a time as ever to begin memorizing them, starting with the open string, twelfth fret, and 7th fret. Even if you only knew those spots you'd simplify the process of counting up or down to figure out note names on the frets between.

Sharps and Flats

Let's pick a harder key like B flat. We want to find the lowest position we can use to play B flat chords with our CAGED forms. If we start counting up from the open sixth string E, we find that the first B flat on the sixth string doesn't occur until fret six. It's possible to play a G form chord and use the frets below fret six so that we are playing in third position (frets three, four, five, and six).

```
E ─┼───┼───┼───┼───┼───┼───┼───┼───┼───┼───┼───┼
B ─┼───┼───┼───┼───┼───┼───┼───┼───┼───┼───┼───┼
G ─┼───┼───┼───┼───┼───┼───┼───┼─●─┼───┼───┼───┼
D ─┼─●─┼───┼─●─┼───┼─●─┼───┼─●─┼─●─┼───┼─●─┼─●─┼
A ─┼───┼───┼───┼───┼───┼───┼───┼───┼───┼───┼───┼
E ─┼───┼───┼───┼───┼─●─┼───┼───┼───┼───┼───┼───┼
    F       G       A  Bb
```

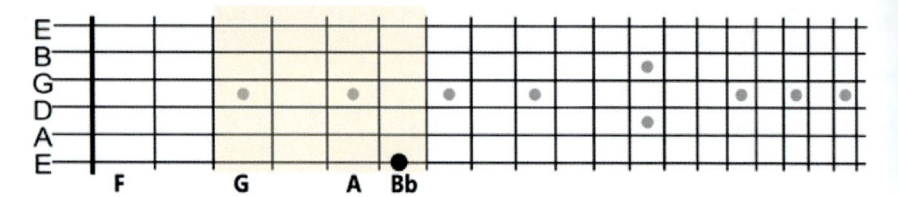

But there might still be a lower position so let's look at the fifth string. Counting up from open fifth string A we find a B flat right away on fret one.

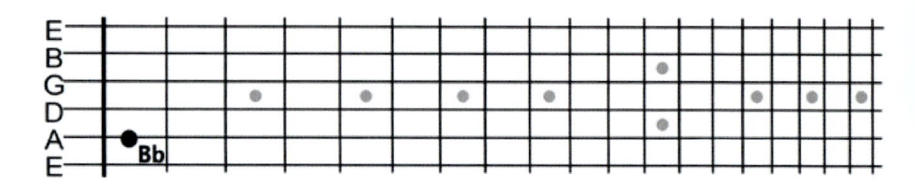

```
E ─┼───┼───┼───┼───┼───┼───┼───┼───┼───┼───┼───┼
B ─┼───┼───┼───┼───┼───┼───┼───┼───┼───┼───┼───┼
G ─┼───┼───┼─●─┼───┼─●─┼───┼─●─┼───┼─●─┼───┼───┼
D ─┼───┼───┼───┼───┼───┼───┼───┼─●─┼───┼───┼───┼
A ─●─┼───┼───┼───┼───┼───┼───┼───┼───┼───┼───┼
E ─┼───┼───┼───┼───┼───┼───┼───┼───┼───┼───┼───┼
   Bb
```

There are two forms we could use to play chords with roots on the fifth string: A or C. The C form can be ruled out right away. It would fall off the neck because we're only on the first fret. That leaves the A form. So we start with the A form on the first fret and cycle through the CAGED series the same way we did in the previous examples using the pivot point method to find each higher position.

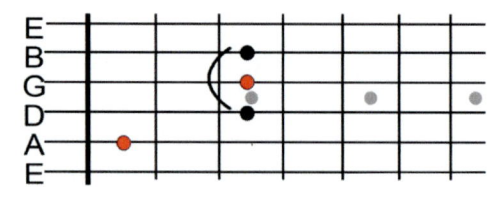

```
E ─┼───┼───┼───┼───┼───┼───┼
B ─┼───┼───┼─●─┼───┼───┼───┼
G ─┼───┼───┼─●─┼───┼─●─┼─●─┼
D ─┼───┼───┼─●─┼───┼───┼───┼
A ─┼─●─┼───┼───┼───┼───┼───┼
E ─┼───┼───┼───┼───┼───┼───┼
```

This process is going to be tedious for a while until you start to remember where to find the common keys you're going to use most often. Just keep in mind that five of the keys are really easy and start memorizing the next most common ones like F and B.

Chapter 2: Chords Become Scales

The primary objective of this whole effort with the CAGED system is to get to the point where you can "see" how to play in a key at any point on the neck. As you get more familiar with this system it expands beyond major keys to include minor keys and modes. The limitations of playing in scale pattern "boxes" simply dissolve. But it doesn't happen all at once.

First, you need to see the boxes, or scale forms, in the five positions, and only in major keys. We do this by associating a major scale pattern with each of the five chord shapes we just used in Chapter 1. Sometimes the associations between the chord and scale shape are very intuitive and obvious, like with the C form. Other times they will seem like a bit of stretch (looking at you, D form, as usual).

Matching the Shapes

E form

Each chord has a corresponding scale shape. If you've been playing for a while you've come across at least one of these, probably the E form. It's usually the first closed-position major scale you play after you've gotten a taste of scales in the open position. We'll start with this one, just to avoid falling in a rut by always starting on the C form. Notice that the scale uses a different finger to play the root.

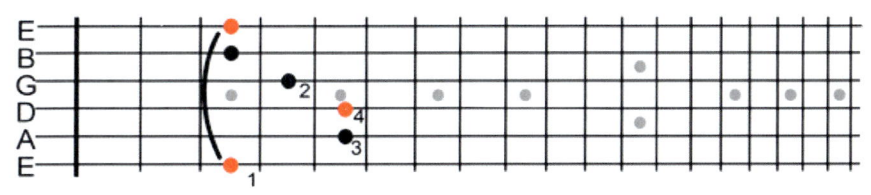

x = notes below the root

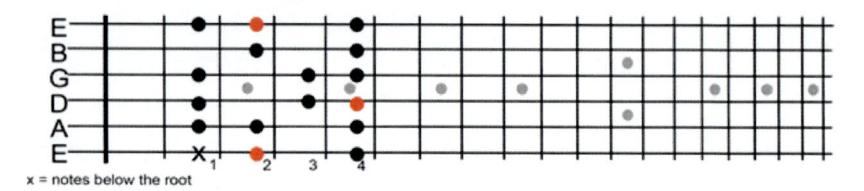

Here you're playing a G major chord and G major scale with the E forms. The rest of the forms are presented here in the key of G with some notes on the relationship between the chords and the scales.

A note on practicing scales

Before you go too far with scales we want to make sure you're practicing them correctly. There's some debate about the value of practicing scales too much but I'm an advocate of using repetitive scale practice as long as you're doing more than just running mindlessly up and down. We'll talk more about this in Chapter 3. For now, let's just make sure you are doing the up and down part correctly.

> Start from the lowest root.
> Play up the scale to the highest available note in the position
> Keep the rhythm consistent. If you have to slow down for the hard parts you're going too fast
> At the highest note turn around and go back to the lowest root
> If there are more notes available below the root play down to the lowest available note
> Play back up and stop on the lowest root where you started

D form

The D form is always the outlier. When we compare the D form scale to the chord we see a number of discrepancies. First, the root has moved to the sixth string. This means it starts from the same note as the E and G forms, but with a focus on a slightly higher part of the neck than the E form. Next, it has more stretching involved than the other forms. To top it off the chord shape doesn't even live completely inside the scale shape the way all the other ones do. The top of the triangle pokes out of the position.

But! I will say that this scale shape is incredibly useful. I really love doing arpeggios and string skipping with this shape. It's just a lot of fun to play with once you get the hang of it. It's also the form that is closest to the forms found in the next most common system for playing scales, the three-notes-per-string system.

A note about stretching

You'll see in this form and some others that there are more frets involved than you have fingers. In other words, one finger has to cover two frets. These stretch fingers will always be finger one or finger four. In this example playing a G major scale with the D form we need to cover frets three through 7. The first finger will play all the notes on frets three and four.

It's important to note that your hand should be placed on the neck as if you were playing in *fourth* position, not third. Fingers two, three, and four, should hold their place on frets five, six, and seven. When you need to play one of the stretch notes on the third fret the first finger should reach down while the rest of the fingers try to maintain their placement over their "home" frets.

If the fourth finger is doing the stretching you hold fingers one, two, and three over their frets and reach with only the fourth finger. Don't move the whole hand to try to reach these notes.

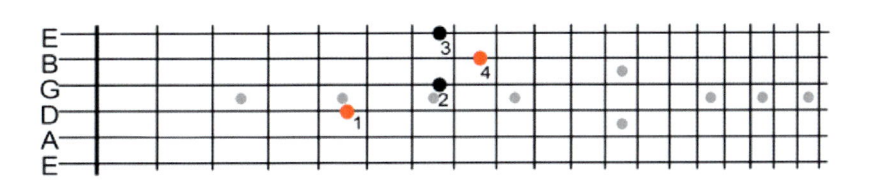

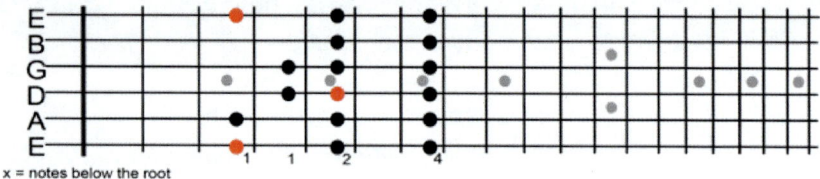

x = notes below the root

C form

The C form will probably be easy for you. There isn't much to say about it except that it has a lot of notes available below the root.

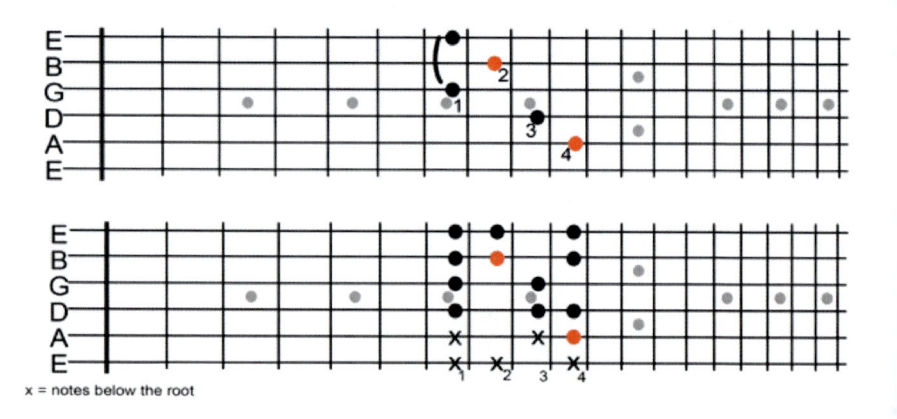

x = notes below the root

A form

A form has a lot of similarity to the E form. Just watch out for the stretch on the first string. And if you're playing all the way down to the very lowest note below the root it shows up again there on the sixth string.

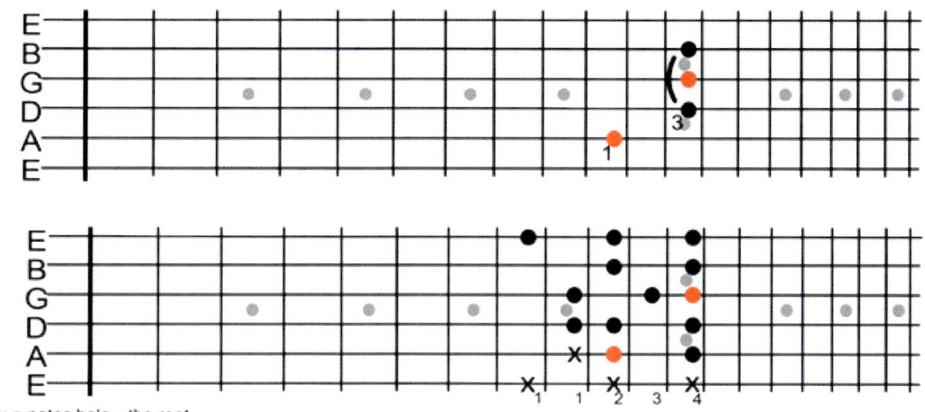

x = notes below the root

G form

If we were to skip ahead and look at the pentatonic variation of this shape in Chapter 4 you'd recognize it immediately. The seven note version here is a bit more difficult, but very useful. There's a very clear relationship between the chord and scale.

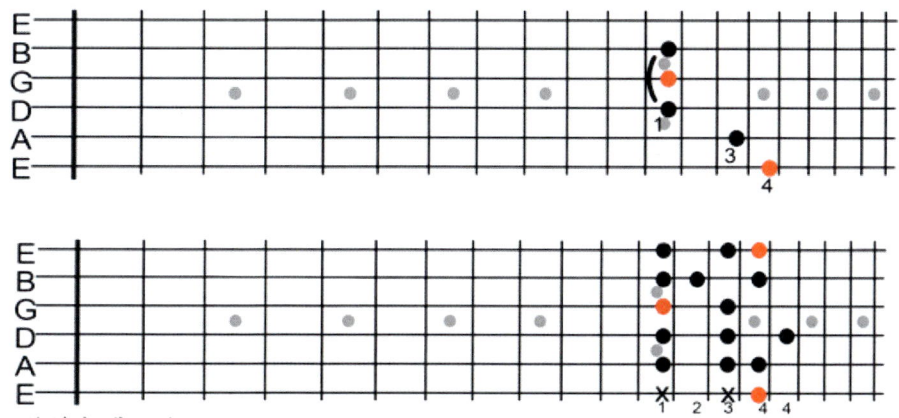

x = notes below the root

Chapter 3: How to Practice

We're past the hard part. Now you know all there is to know about the five forms. But we're far from done. What remains is knowing how to drill them without getting bored, being able to use them functionally in real world situations, and understanding how to extract the right parts to derive arpeggios and other scales from the full forms. And let's not forget connecting them fluidly so you don't feel like you're still stuck inside boxes!

Drilling

Running through pattern based variations and sequences provides all the drilling you will ever need. I will give you examples of the most obvious ways to do this. If you are obsessed with practicing scales you can probably come up with quite a few more.

The notated examples for Chapter 3 are found in their complete form on my website because they won't be much good to you on a small device screen.

http://danmylotte.com/guitarwisdom/unlock/

The video version of this course deals with the drills in some detail:

https://goo.gl/zpA6n8

Can I Solo Yet?

You could, but I recommend you get past the pentatonic and arpeggio sections first. I have an improvisation course on YouTube that walks you through a process that matches notes and scales to chords and progressions using the five position system:

https://goo.gl/P0QXXv

It builds improvisation skills from the ground up, starting from arpeggios, moving to pentatonics and finally seven note scales at the end. At the end of this book I'll walk you through a modified version of this same process.

What you can and should do with them now is play other melodies, just not improvised ones. This is going to feel like going backwards but I have to emphasize that this one step will really cement your understanding of the instrument more than a lot of scale drills.

Twinkle, Twinkle

Start with a known melody. Your first attempts should be melodies that are very familiar and easy. It may seem ridiculous but use nursery rhymes. Use a piece of a vocal melody from a song you know well or a guitar hook. Whatever it is, just make sure it's *diatonic*, meaning it uses only notes from the major scale. If it has any chromatic notes it defeats the purpose of the exercise.

Pick one of the five scale forms and play your melody strictly inside that shape with no cheating. You know how guitar players cheat. They go looking way up and down a single string for notes and say, "oh, it sounds right." This is precisely what we're trying to get away from with this whole five position system.

If playing your example melodies is easy, that's great. If it's not, *you should try to figure out where the note is going to be before you hunt around and make a bunch of mistakes using trial and error.* This makes it into a kind of ear training exercise. You are trying to integrate the separate aspects of learning and processing that are going on between your ears, your mind, and your fingers. Your ears know what note they need to hear. Your mind and fingers are probably not as certain where to find it. Carefully consider the distances involved and try to gauge how far up or down the scale you'll need to go to find it. This is the mind part. Now try to see where this note is likely to be in the pattern you chose. This is the finger part.

Music students spend a lot of semesters in courses that are specifically designed to build these skills. Believe it or not, you can approximate a lot of that study just by trying to play Twinkle, Twinkle Little Star (for example, in the Key of F# using the A form scale). Just don't barrel through it. If you make a mistake, instead of immediately banging into the next note up or down, try to hear how far off you were and gauge what the right note might be. This will teach you a lot more than just plowing through it with trial and error.

I suspect you're going to be frustrated by this process, even if you use a seemingly easy tune. What it reveals is not that you're a hopeless case of no talent. It really gets the the bottom of the problem with the guitar's interface: it's not intuitive; it's irregular; It doesn't give you a lot visual cues for where things should be found. The guitar was clearly designed to be a chord instrument first.

A person with zero experience on the piano could probably do this more effectively on a keyboard than you're going to be on the guitar for a while, because it's a much more obvious interface. But with consistent practice the intuition will develop and you'll find you know how to go "up a fifth from scale degree three in the G form" (or whatever) with much less trouble than when you started.

Chapter 4: Pentatonic

Now we're going to begin a process of reducing the number of notes in the shapes to extract other useful musical sounds from the major scale, starting with pentatonics. I don't want to clutter up this text with too much detail about the theory behind pentatonics. If you want a slightly longer (but still very brief and introductory) explanation of why they are what they are then take a look at my lesson on pentatonics:

https://goo.gl/YMSWzP

A half step is the distance of one fret to the next. This happens twice in the major scale. To make a major scale into pentatonic (technically, "major pentatonic") we just take out the two half steps.

We're left with patterns that always have only two notes on each string, making for very easy playing and memorization.

E form pentatonic

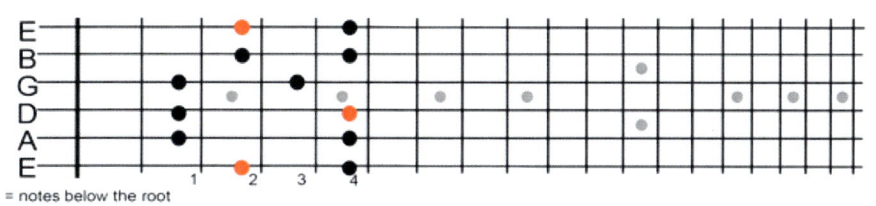

x = notes below the root

The D form requires a bit of explanation. It's possible to start it on the same note that we used in the seven note scale. But I prefer to show it without. This is one case where I leave it up to you to decide if you want to use my fingering. There are a few ways you could do it.

x = notes below the root

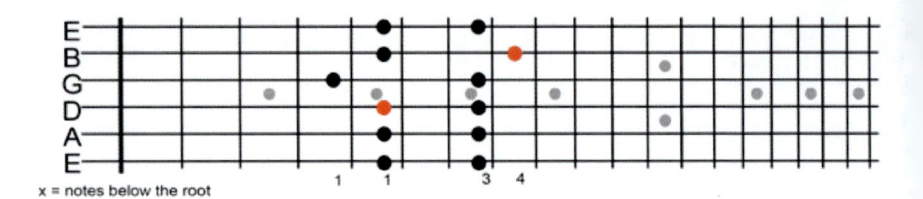

C form pentatonic

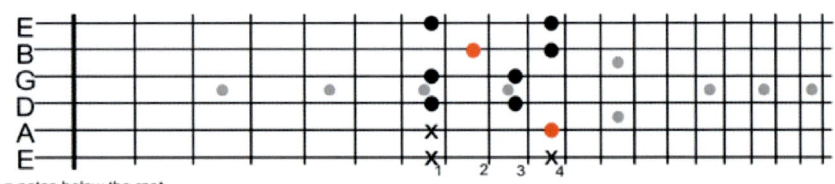

x = notes below the root

A form pentatonic

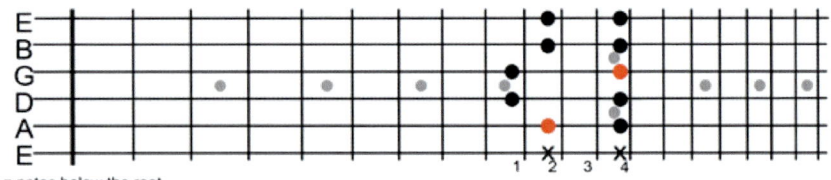

x = notes below the root

G form pentatonic. Note this is the form that almost every student learns first, although it's typically presented as a minor scale with the root on the first finger.

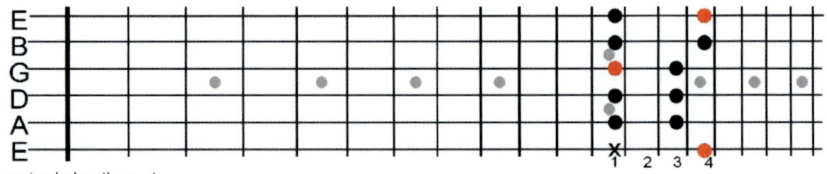

x = notes below the root

A note about fingerings

When it comes to the seven note scale patterns from Chapter 2 I'm extremely strict about learning the fingerings as I've presented them. There are relatively few ways in which they could be altered and in almost all cases any alterations would likely be a detriment to playing them successfully. However, some people like to change them and I don't discourage this IF you have already learned them the way they're presented here.

When it comes to the pentatonic versions, though, you have a lot more room to modify the fingerings. I do still suggest that you focus on playing them as shown in these diagrams before you make too many changes. After you've gotten a feel for these shapes you can probably find at least one or two spots that you would prefer to play differently (especially with that troublesome D form). You'll find a great many players that don't use finger four at all when playing pentatonics.

What I really want to see is the patterns sinking in and becoming second nature. This will only happen successfully when they are played with the same fingerings every time. So if you're going to change them, write them down and be consistent. Much later on you may no longer even need to finger them consistently (or even think much about them at all), but for the purposes of learning and memorizing I feel that consistency is necessary.

Making Fluid Connections: the Escalator

It's time to take an important step toward getting out of the "box" feeling that comes from playing too much in one position. This is always a big complaint of people who think they don't want to use scale patterns. What they are missing is the realization that the patterns can eventually become more of a mental framework than a physical one. The easiest way to start achieving this mobility is to identify the places where one pattern can translate to the next with an easy finger slide.

I think of this as the Escalator Shift because you can slide up and down (the escalator) between positions (the different floors you can get off and on) and spend as long as you like in each place. All you need to start is to know where the easiest locations are for the finger slide. We're looking for a place where a two fret slide will land you in the new position. There are lots of them.

But before we make an exhaustive study of every spot and diagram them all, let's look at the simplest lick you can build with the escalator idea. It's actually just a scale that shifts through all the positions using this finger slide concept.

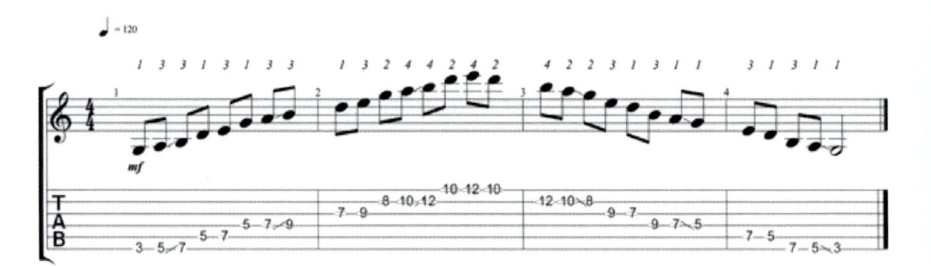

```
♩ = 120
     1 3 3 1 3 1 3 3    1 3 2 4 4 2 4 2    4 2 2 3 1 3 1 1    3 1 3 1 1

T|------------------------------------------------10-12-10---------------------------|
A|-------------------------------8-10-12-----12-10-8--------------------|
B|--------------5-7-9------7-9--------------------9-7-----9-7-5-------7-5---------|
 |-3-5-7------------------------------------------------------------7-5-3-|
mf
```

Notice we don't spend too long in any one position with this scale. But now imagine that instead of shifting quickly to the next position you instead "get off the escalator" and start playing more notes from that position's pattern. You'll need some other "exit points" to make the escalator shift besides the ones in the scale lick above. Here are all the places that match the criteria for where you can make a similar shift between positions.

Shifting from the E form to D form, keep in mind that the quirky D form fingerings mean you need to do a little maneuvering once you shift. This will happen in other positions as well.

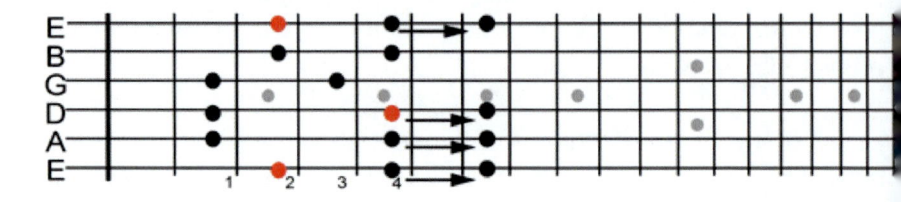

From D form to C form:

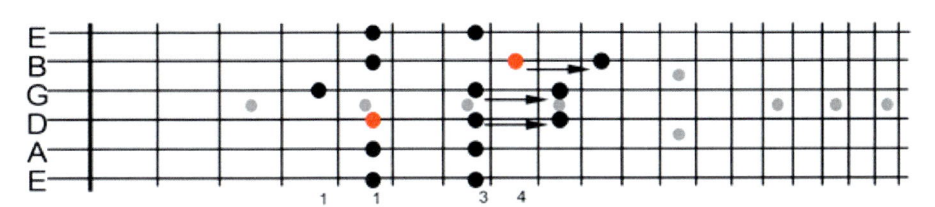

C form to A form:

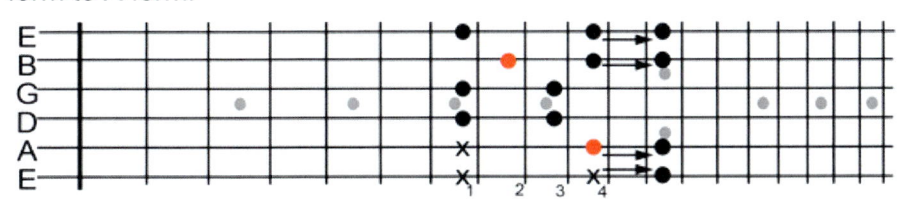

A form to G form:

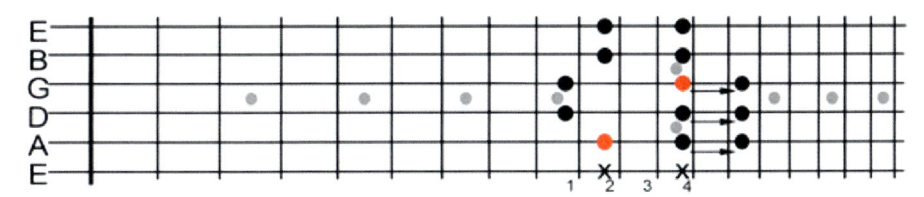

G form to E form:

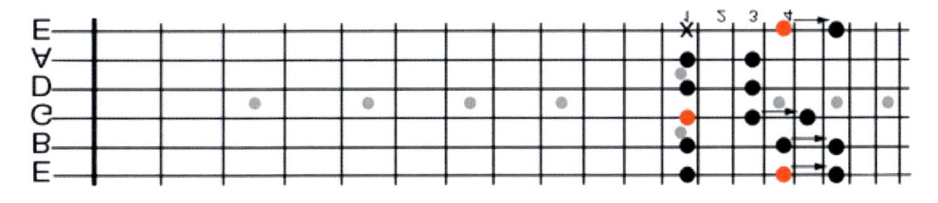

Let's be clear about a few things. I'm not saying these are the only places you can move between positions. I just find them to be the simplest and clearest places. I believe they're worth studying.

When you want to shift down you just reverse the arrows. But use the fingering from the higher form. In other words, higher fingers shift up and lower fingers shift down.

Chapter 5: Arpeggios

Keeping with the theme of taking notes away, let's get rid of two more and we'll be left with triad arpeggios. Arpeggiating a chord means you break out the notes into a melody instead of playing them simultaneously as a chord sound. The Guitar Wisdom series on triads might help you out:

https://goo.gl/KtNfBm

There's also one on diatonic triads:

https://goo.gl/dX8kdA

The odd part about playing arpeggios is that despite having fewer notes than pentatonic scales, it's likely you'll find them more difficult to play, and especially to remember, than pentatonic shapes. This is because they are much less regular. Now we no longer have two notes on every string. But it's worth investing some time to get the hang of these.

E form:

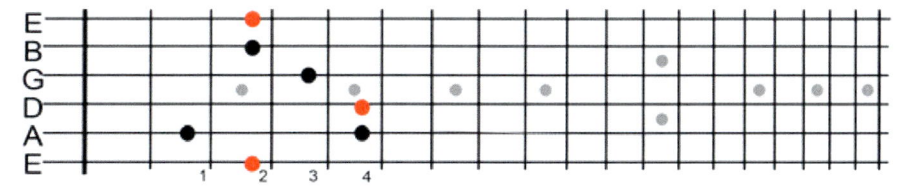

I find arpeggios to be the single most instructive device for understanding the way the guitar works. If you spend time learning them and really discerning the relationships between the notes in the position and the different positions to each other, you'll come away with a more intuitive sense of the instrument's layout and quirks.

D form requires some explanation. The form I'm giving you here is much more useful than it would be if I stuck with the form the pentatonic uses. The stretching can be uncomfortable and the string skipping takes some getting used to. But I promise you will come to love this shape.

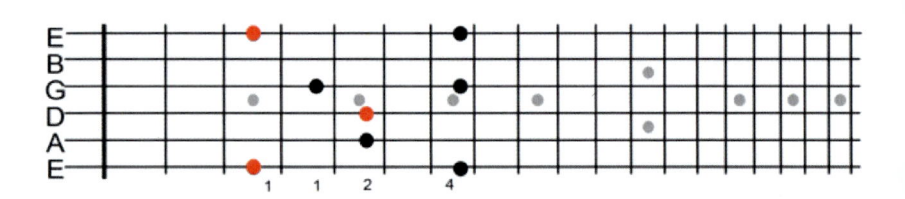

C form:

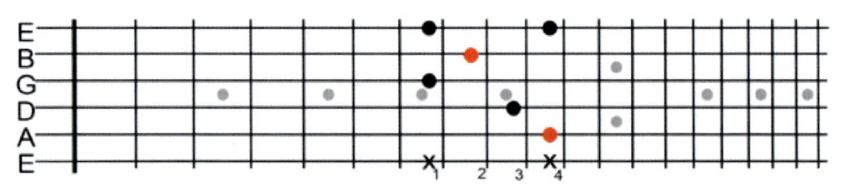

A form:

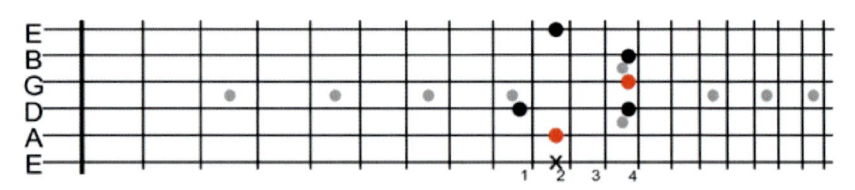

G form:

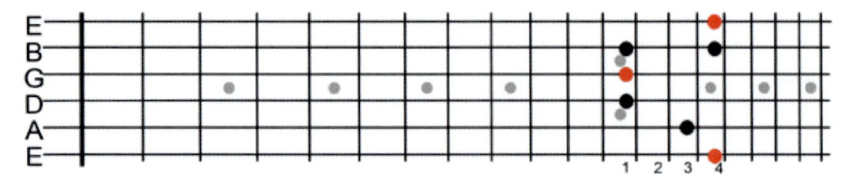

Why no minor?

At this point you may have started to wonder why I don't talk about minor scales or chords. There are several reasons. First and foremost, you don't need any more scale shapes to play minor scales. It's important to understand that these 5 shapes are the only ones you need to learn. To get minor scales out of them, you just learn a little bit of scale theory and, *voila*, they are minor. This is a million times easier than learning more patterns.

For example, here are the pentatonic scales rewritten to show the minor roots. You can see that all we've done is move the root to a new note, the sixth. Start them from this note and they sound minor. Much easier than learning more patterns!

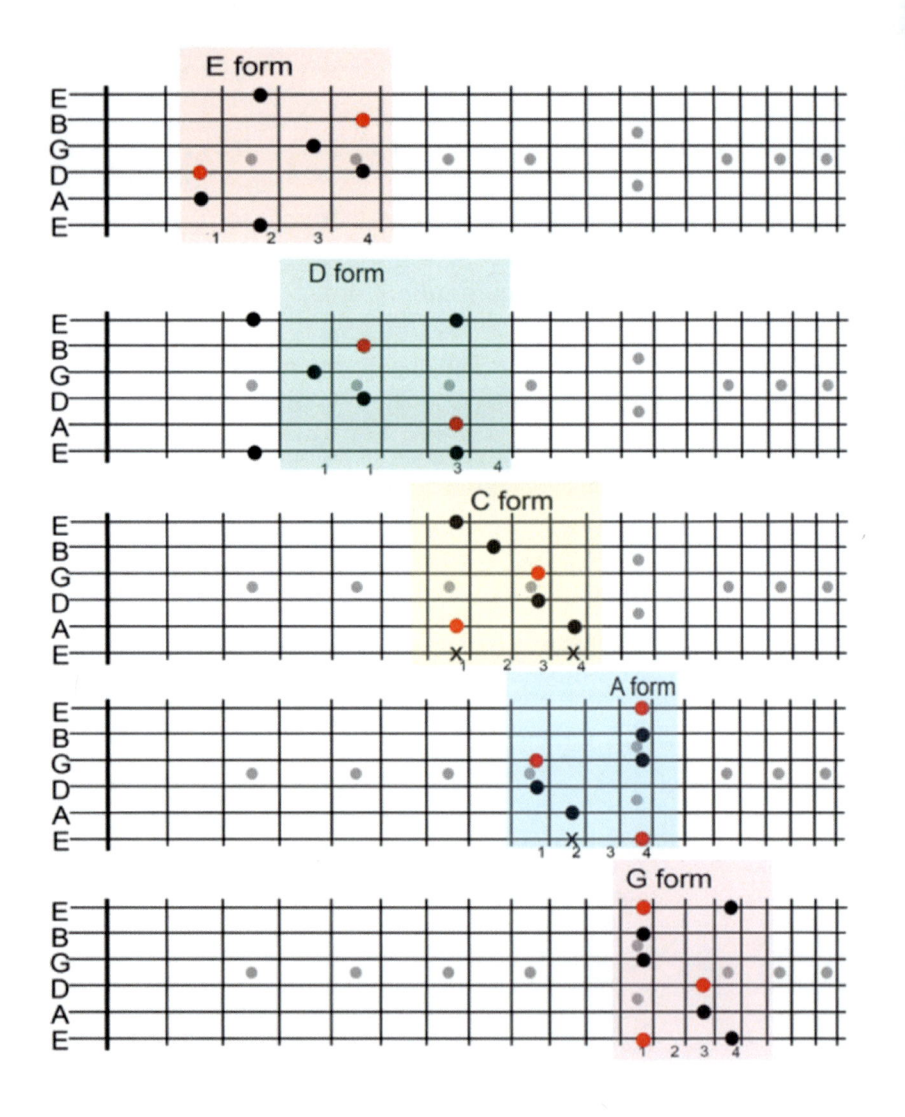

There are only a small handful of things you need different shapes for, and even then I think it's still easier to think of them as modifications of the five positions instead of wholly different things. The truly different sounds would be things like harmonic and melodic minor, diminished, whole tone, etc. Those scales have fundamental differences from the major scale.

True minor keys do not happen as often as you might think. A minor key and a minor mode are not really the same thing. For everything you know that's "minor" only a handful are minor key. The rest are minor modes. Minor modes can be played with the CAGED forms. The remaining true minor key music will still only require adjustment when you get to a V dominant chord, which is outside the scope of this book. My point is that these forms, combined with a growing body of knowledge about music and how it works, will be more than ample to meet the needs of nearly every modern guitar player.

But this chapter is about arpeggios, and that is one case where we want to make sure that we *do* have a pattern for the minor side of things. They are not just a reworking of the major arpeggios so let's take a look. If you compare these to the minor pentatonics above, you can see they follow the same principle as the reduction of the major pentatonics to major triad arpeggios. The only difference is that one of the eliminated notes is different than it was for the major triad.

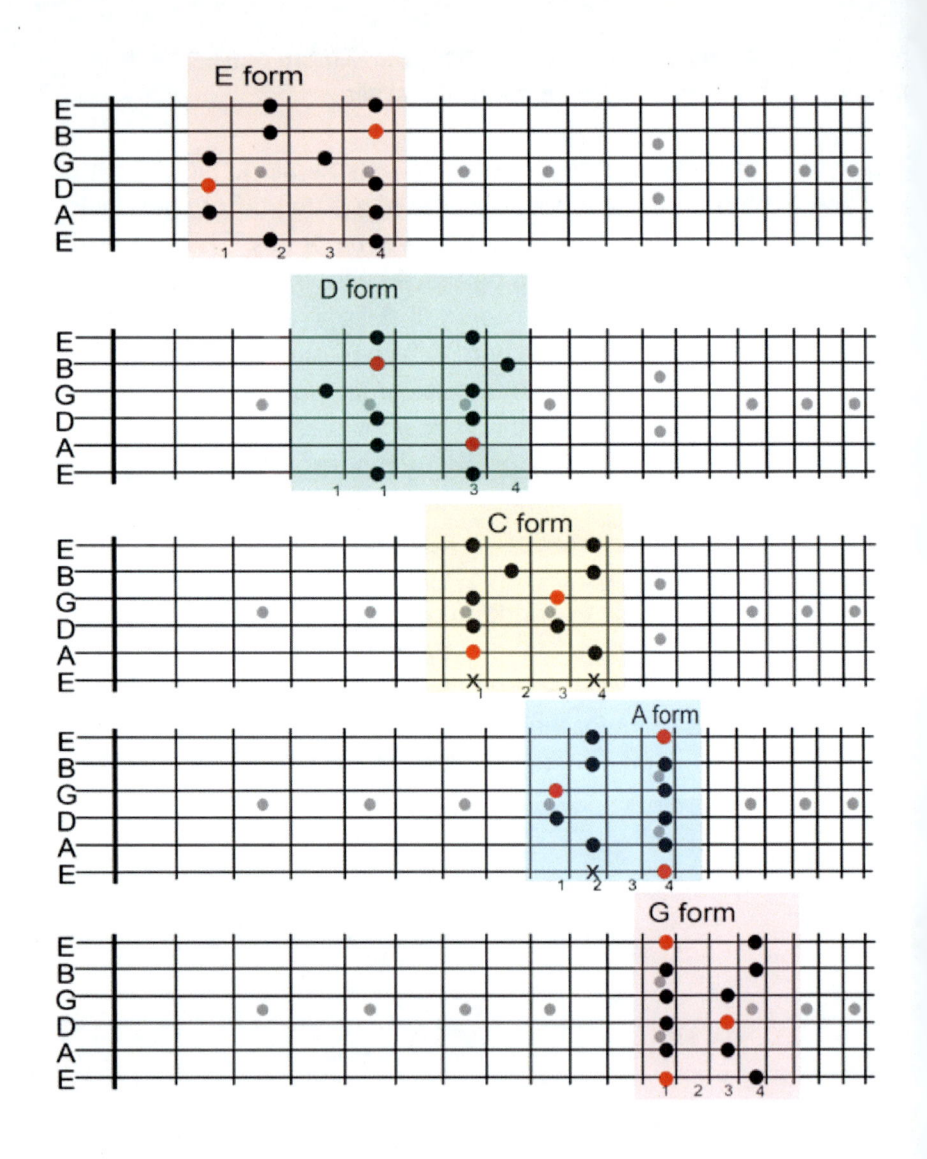

There are plenty of other ways you could be playing arpeggios in these or any position, but these are the ones that are most closely related to the pentatonic forms so they're included here for the sake of trying to be as thorough as possible with the five positions.

Chapter 6: Making It Stick

That's it for patterns. I suggest limiting your memorization of shapes to what I've shown you here: five major scale shapes and the reductions of those scales to pentatonic and triad arpeggios. Now comes the lengthy process of drilling these shapes until you don't need diagrams for reference. The time needed for this will vary a great deal from player to player. But it shouldn't be long before you can begin to apply them in more real world scenarios.

Improvisation is one of our main end goals for this course, but it's a much bigger topic than just throwing some scale shapes around and saying "go!" My Guitar Wisdom video course for improvisation demonstrates methods for applying the CAGED forms to chord progressions for students that have begun to internalize the shapes already:

https://goo.gl/3QnZkC

To get closer to that point, we can apply some of the same concepts at a simpler level.

Accompanying yourself

If you don't already have a way of recording chord accompaniments to improvise over it's time to acquire this ability. Yes, the internet is full of play-along videos but they will rarely be tailored to the needs of very targeted practice like what we require here. You don't need an elaborate home studio. In most cases, a phone app that records audio coming out of your amplifier could be a suitable solution. You just need to be able to hear chord sound and play over it.

For all of the following suggestions you are going to record a single major chord sound. The tempo and rhythm you use for this is up to you, but it can be helpful to play to a metronome or drum machine and strum a simple rhythm in time with that beat.

Reveille

I mentioned earlier that most people will find it harder to play arpeggios than pentatonics. And using only three note is limiting, yes. But you can still make music with triad arpeggios. That's what bugle calls like Reveille do because the bugle can only play a triad arpeggio.

Using your chord accompaniment in whatever key you like, improvise using only triad arpeggios in one position at a time. At first you'll want to play up and down the notes in order. This will get tiresome quickly so next you should start playing them out of order. Give it some rhythmic variation and you can keep yourself busy with these for a while.

This will likely not be the most rewarding musical experience you've ever had, but there is a lot of value in getting these arpeggio shapes really deeply embedded in your fingers. Change the key frequently so you don't get too stuck on any one part of the neck. You can do the same thing with the minor triads.

Once is not enough! There's no possible way you can practice these in only one session. There are twelve keys, five patterns, and both major/minor triad types. That's 120 things to work on. While it's not crucial that you cover every single one of those possibilities, you should be coming back to these many times and reinforcing them over an extended period.

Blues

Pentatonics are next, and the concept is identical. You're adding two more notes so you should feel a lot more satisfied with the sounds you can make with just this small addition. When you get to the minor side of the pentatonics you can try substituting blues progressions if you're bored with the single chords. For example, instead of A minor you can play an A blues progression while you improvise A minor pentatonic.

Getting out of the box

Feel free at this point to start introducing the shifts from Chapter 4 to begin erasing the boundaries between the positions. Shift as much as you want, but pay attention to the roots in your destination position. Knowing the major roots is more important, but if you're doing the blues accompaniment it's the minor roots you're looking for.

All Seven Notes

Of course we're going to want to do the same thing with the seven note major scales. While more notes make for more interesting melodies, the re-introduction of the half steps creates the possibility of playing notes that have dissonant relationships to the accompanying chord. It's more important than ever, then, to make sure your ears are telling you what they want to hear next, and for your mind and fingers to attempt the discovery of that note.

Minor chords will work here, too. Just remember where the roots were for the minor pentatonics. They are the same root for a seven note minor scale.

One Chord, So Bored

I'm sure you're tired of that one chord accompaniment. There's nothing wrong with adding more chords, but it introduces all kinds of variables that make your practice session less about learning the CAGED forms and more about improvisation or theory practice. I'm a big proponent of compartmentalized practice. If I'm drilling shapes,

I'm not worried about my technique. If I'm practicing technique, I'm not getting hung up on how musical I sound. And so on.

If you understand how chords work together in a key, go ahead and make more interesting chord progressions. My Guitar Wisdom series on diatonic triads can help you out here:

https://goo.gl/dX8kdA

This will give you an idea of why chords go together in a key. Or you could try out the improvisation course if think you have a handle on the forms:

https://goo.gl/P0QXXvv

The first lesson is about understanding the context of the key you're in so you know where to play the five positions on the neck. It's a great next step for anyone who is developing familiarity with the CAGED system.

Further Study

There are a million great resources out there to expand on what has been covered in this book. Hopefully you will interpret them with greater understanding and objectivity now that you have more insight into the guitar's complex interface. A lot of the material out there is presented by people who know just enough to be dangerous. They may actually have something worth sharing, but not have the depth of knowledge to connect it to fundamental concepts.

Some people find it helpful to write out the shapes themselves into blank diagrams in a variety of keys. This will certainly reinforce memorization and the ability to locate roots. A similar process involves writing out notes and/or tabs for the scales, although this is considerably more time consuming.

An exhaustive study of the five positions across most keys can be found in the Berklee Modern Method for Guitar: Volume Two. But be prepared to digest a lot of written notation. The exercises are very useful if you have recently learned these patterns, but they are written in standard notation only.

As you can see, I'm not interested in telling you what to play. There's enough of this material out there already. I've tried to limit this text to explaining the five position system as thoroughly as possible. It's up to you to figure out what to do with it!

Made in the USA
Las Vegas, NV
14 October 2021